When Someone Dies

A Book about Death for Kids who are Curious or who are Experiencing a Death

Written and Illustrated by
Laura Camerona, CCLS

A
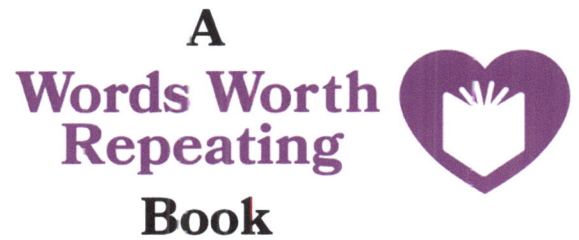
Book

Copyright © 2021 by Laura Camerona

This book is intended to be read to a child by a trusted adult.

The advice and words within may not be suitable for every child or every situation. It is suggested that the reader looks through the tips before reading this book with childern. In especially stressful or complex situations, this author suggests the involvement of a mental health professional.

Book best suited for children ages 4-12.

No part of this publication may be reproduced, stored in a retrieval system, or transmitted in any form or by any means, electronic, mechanical, photocopying, recording, or otherwise, without the written permission of the author. Specific requests may be sent to laura@wordsworthrepeating.com.

ISBN 978-1-7367884-0-0 Paperback

www.wordsworthrepeating.com

WWR's Tips and Ideas for Reading this Book with a Group:

-There are many personal questions in this book. Do not require that kids answer the questions outloud.
- As a group, have a conversation before you read the book. Talk about how the group can make it a safe place to share.
-If you feel that sharing aloud will not be appopriate for your group, give them time to think about their answers and encourage them to talk about it with their caregivers or other trusted adults.
-Follow this book with some sort of activity that gives kids a chance to reflect on their feelings and questions. Writing and creating artwork are great ways for children to express their feelings. For more ideas, check out the blog titled: 10 Expressive Grief Activities at www.wordsworthrepeating.com. Again, let their creations be private, if they wish.

WWR's Tips for Reading this Book One-on-One with a Child:

-Follow the child's lead. If they aren't in the mood to read the book, save it for another moment.
-Stop and answer questions. If in the middle of the book, your child wants to talk about one part of the book or one question that they have, set the book aside and focus on that.
-Often, bedtime isn't the best time for books that children might have questions about. It can lead to trouble sleeping. The first time you read this book with your child, avoid reading it just before bed.
-Use this book as a prompt for more discussion. There are lots of unanswered questions in this book. You can follow your child's answers with "Why do you feel this way?" or "What makes you think that?" Share your answers with your child and explain to them why you feel that way.
-Remember that 'magical thinking' is common in young children. They may like making up other possibilities. This is okay and normal.
-Don't expect a certain outword reaction from your child. It is okay if your child doesn't show the emotions that you might expect. It is also okay if your child is sad. Sad is an okay feeling. Support them by sharing that death makes you sad sometimes too. Let them decide if they want to be done talking about it or if they would like to talk about it more.
-If your child asks questions or reacts in a way that you don't feel comfortable with, reach out to a counselor at their school or their medical provider to get a referral for additional support. Most communities have organizations that support grieving families and children.
-More resources are available at www.wordsworthrepeating.com. Check out the blog on our website for further activites that support grieving children. Also, get more information about creating a customized book about a person in your child's life who has died.

Dedicated to all that spend their lives supporting families experiencing their hardest days, some of who helped edit this book.

Dedicated to families, who are taking things day-by-day, together.

Dedicated to my own three "question-askers". Your questions, no doubt, made this book better.

Do you know what happens when someone dies?

Some people don't like to talk about death because they think it is sad or scary.

It is okay to feel sad sometimes.

Sometimes when we know more about things, they seem less scary.

When people, animals, or plants die, that means that they stop living.

People have lived as long as 117 years. A Bristlecone pine tree has lived as long as 5,000 years, but all living things die eventually.

For a person or an animal, this means that the heart stops beating and bringing blood to the rest of the body. The lungs stop breathing. The brain doesn't work anymore and can not send messages to the rest of the body.

For a plant, this means that it stops bringing water up from its roots, and it stops turning sunshine into energy to grow.

Once someone or something is dead, it can not become alive again.

Sometimes people get hurt badly, and they stop breathing or their heart stops for a short time. Doctors can help their bodies start working again. This is not the same thing as being dead.

When someone is dead, he or she can not feel pain.

Once a person dies, they do not need their body anymore. People often tell their loved ones where they would like their body to be put after they die. If not, family and friends decide. Then, someone called a funeral director helps the person's family make plans for the person's body.

Some people are buried underground in a special box called a casket or a coffin. Often they are buried next to other people that were in their family.

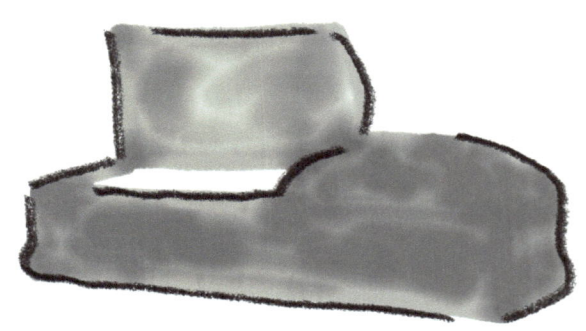

Some people are cremated. Cremated means that a specially trained person gets the body very hot, so that it turns into ashes. Remember that this does not hurt the person because their body is dead.

A person's ashes can be buried, spread in the person's favorite place, or kept. If the ashes are kept, they can be put in a container called an urn or put inside a piece of jewelry or artwork.

Some people choose, before they die, to be "organ donors". This means that doctors can take parts of the person's body, after he or she dies, and use them to help people who are sick or injured. For example, there are times when a doctor can take a heart from a dead body and put it in a living person whose heart is very sick to help the person live a longer and healthier life.

Often the decisions made about a person's body are affected by their religion or their culture. Certain parts of the world tend to follow certain traditions.

Some people choose to donate their body. This means that the body is given to doctors and scientists so that they can study it and learn more about how to take care of the human body.

There are many reasons that people can die, but most people live long lives.

People can die because they have a very serious illness or disease. Most illnesses and diseases do not make people die.

People can die because parts of their body stop working. This usually happens when someone is old or his or her body isn't working the way it is supposed to.

People can die because their body gets badly damaged. This could happen if someone got in a bad accident.

There are lots of people in our community that work hard to keep you, your family, and your friends safe and healthy. These people include firefighters, police officers, paramedics, doctors, nurses, teachers, and even your parents!

But, did you know that each person is more than just a body? We each have something called a soul. A soul is not something you can see with your eyes. Your soul makes you who you are.

Your soul is the part of you that loves a favorite color, prefers certain activities, and loves certain people.

What does your soul love?

People around the world believe different things about what happens to a person's soul when they die.

Some people believe that a person's soul goes to Heaven or Paradise. In Heaven, a person is with God and other friends or family who have died.

Some people believe that the soul becomes a Guardian Angel. The Guardian Angel looks after his or her friends and family.

Some people believe that where a soul goes after death is decided by how the person lived their life.

Some people believe that the person's soul is reborn as another animal or person.

Some people see death as a mystery.

Another word for a soul is a spirit.

Talk to your parents or other people in your life about what they believe. What do you believe?

The memories of people who have died can affect the world, by impacting the things their loved ones say and do. Memories are very important.

Often, people that we love make us feel good. If someone we love dies, it is important to remember how we felt when we were with them.

We learn a lot about life from the people we love. We can still feel people that have died affecting our lives, when we remember the things that they taught us.

The way people continue to affect the world after they die is called their "legacy". A person's legacy can be lots of things, like how people remember the person, lessons they taught those around them, the new ideas they brought to the world, or how their money helps people after they die.

You can help yourself remember things about someone who has died.

You can write down your favorite memories or have a grown-up help you.

You can look at old pictures of the person who died.

You can use their favorite recipes to make food that reminds you of them.

You can ask your parents or other grownups to tell you stories about someone who has died.

People around the world use different celebrations and rituals to remember their loved one's who have died.

Almost all countries and cultures have a day set aside for visiting gravesites and celebrating the dead.

Some people make food that remind them of their loved ones.

Some people celebrate the Day of the Dead or All Soul's Day and set out special things that welcome their loved one's souls to come back and visit.

Some people visit their loved ones' gravesites on special days like Memorial Day or on the person's birthday.

Some people in Asia celebrate the Hungry Ghost Festival or a similar holiday called Odon. They believe that the spirits of the dead come to visit them and then they guide the spirits home using floating lanterns.

You don't have to wait for a special day to think about your loved one and their death. You might think about it every single day.

When you think of people you know that have died, you can feel a lot of different things. All of these feelings are okay. The big feelings a person has when someone they loved has died are called "grief".

You could feel happy remembering good memories of the person. You may even laugh.

You could feel sad that your life will be different now that they are gone.

You could feel worried about how your life might change.

You could feel sad that you don't get to spend time with them.

You could feel happy that you had such a special person in your life or you could feel happy that the person isn't suffering anymore.

You could feel mad that your life changed because of the death.

You could forget about it for a while too, and that's okay too.

In some cases, you may not know the person that died. You may still feel sad that you didn't get to know them. You may feel sad that your friends or family are sad.

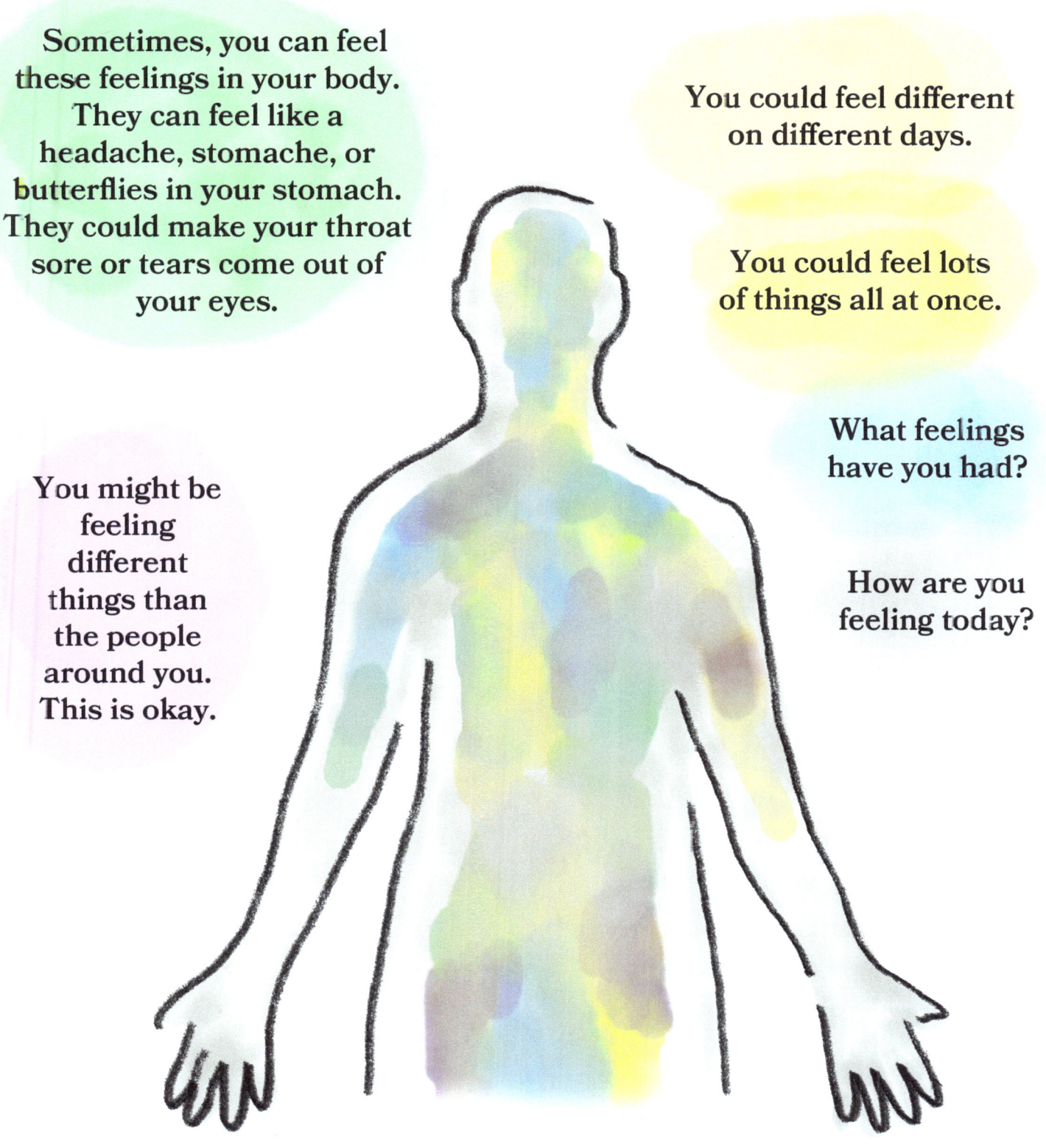

Sometimes, you can feel these feelings in your body. They can feel like a headache, stomache, or butterflies in your stomach. They could make your throat sore or tears come out of your eyes.

You could feel different on different days.

You could feel lots of things all at once.

What feelings have you had?

How are you feeling today?

You might be feeling different things than the people around you. This is okay.

When you are having these feelings, sometimes it helps to tell someone about it. It could be a family member, a friend, a teacher, or a counselor. When you are ready to share, it can really help.

Right after someone dies, many people find that it helps to be with other people who loved or cared for the person who died.

These gatherings can look very different in different cultures. Sometimes, they happen at the family's home. While other times, it takes place at a special building called a funeral home where the funeral director helps plan the gathering. Still other times, the gathering takes place at a church, temple, synagogue, or mosque.

Often times, people gather after a person dies. This gathering can be called a funeral, a wake, or a visitation.

People often share their memories with other people who cared about the person. In many cultures, they pray for the person.

Sometimes, people send flowers to show how important the person was to them or to let the person's friends and family know that they are thinking of them. People also donate money in honor of the person or bring food to the person's closest friends and family.

Sometimes the person's dead body is at this gathering so that people can say "goodbye". If it is at the gathering, it will usually be in a casket. Remember, a casket is the special box that people are buried in.

It is your choice whether you want to visit the body or not. If you choose to, you can talk to the person's body or gently touch the person. You should know their body will feel different. Without life in the body, it will feel cool instead of warm. The body won't feel as soft as when they were alive.

The dead person's eyes will be closed. This may look like they are sleeping, but they are not.

After the gathering, the body is buried in a cemetery, which is an open area where other people are buried.

Being at one of these gatherings can help someone who is sad, not feel alone.

After reading this book, you still probably have questions about death. Lots of people wonder about death. It is okay to ask questions about death and dying.

It is okay if you don't want to think about it a lot or if you think about it all of the time.

If you have questions that you want to ask, but you don't want to ask them right now, you can talk to a counselor, family member, or friend. Choose someone that you feel comfortable talking to.

And, if someone that you love has died, remember that you can still talk to them, even if you can't see them. You can tell everyone about them. You will never forget them. You are special because their memory lives on in you.

In the case of a recent death, each child may need a different explanation based on a variety factors. If needing further information about how to explain a specific death or wanting to give another layer of support to a child, here are some ideas:

💜 Reach out to a counselor or mental health professional that is already in your child's life.

💜 Talk to the child's school or doctor about a referral for another layer of support such as a grief therapist, creative arts therapist, or play therapist in your community.

💜 Contact Words Worth Repeating to work with a child life specialist to create a customized book specifically for your situation. (www.wordsworthrepeating.com)

In addition, here are some tips for explaining and talking about a specific death with a child:

💜 Be honest, but gentle. Some people wonder whether they should tell a child the truth about what happened. If the death directly affects the child, the answer is 'yes'. Word travels quickly in communities and families, and kids listen. It is best for children to find out about things from a trusted adult. Being honest does not mean that you have to be detailed. Use simple words.

💜 Do not put blame on the person who died. As you grieve, you may feel angry with the person who died. This is a natural part of the grieving process, but do not pass this anger on to the child. In situations such as suicide and addiction, it is important for the child to understand the person had a 'sick brain'. Put the focus on the deceased person's sickness that made their brain make choices that they wouldn't have normally. Remind them that what happened does not mean that the person did not love the child. In situations that were not a result of mental health and/or addiction, help children understand when something was an accident.

💜 Help the child feel safe. If it is a situation where the child's living situation will change based on the death, talk to them about this. Let them know that there are adults that love them who will help figure it out. Listen and acknowledge opinions about what they want. Do not promise them anything you can't be sure of. Let them know the plan when there is one.

💜 Follow the child's lead. It is usually best to start with a simple version of what happened. Follow your explanation by asking the child what questions he or she has. If they seem interested but maybe too nervous to ask, you can say something like, "If I was your age, I would wonder _____. Are you wondering that?" Be sure that the child knows that they can be done talking about it at any point.

www.ingramcontent.com/pod-product-compliance
Lightning Source LLC
Chambersburg PA
CBHW042256100526
44589CB00002B/46